HANDS UP

MR. REDD

authorHOUSE®

AuthorHouse™
1663 Liberty Drive
Bloomington, IN 47403
www.authorhouse.com
Phone: 1 (800) 839-8640

Published by AuthorHouse 01/22/2019

ISBN: 978-1-5462-5558-1 (sc)
ISBN: 978-1-5462-5556-7 (hc)
ISBN: 978-1-5462-5557-4 (e)

Library of Congress Control Number: 2018909742

Print information available on the last page.

CONTENTS

1, 2, 3

There is no substitution for learning math facts, and speed is a necessity. Mental math is the key to learning the times tables. Give your students ten problems daily to help them build their mental math skills. Start easy, and build up as they progress. Help your students make connections, e.g., solving for 100 + 100 + 100, then 99+ 99+ 99. Mental math is pure joy and it builds confidence.

4 Guys and a Van-Moving Day

One thing they do not teach you in "teacher school" is that some students can and will talk to ANYONE. Moving day can be a continuing activity for some. In the classroom, a student's neighbor can be an ally or the "enemy". Sometimes you have to change the neighborhoods for your students for them to be successful.

Advertising 101

Okay, you have been chosen to create the hallway bulletin board-I did not say it was an honor, just that you have been picked. Go immediately to the library and to find the latest edition of the teacher's "Mailbox". Don't you dare! Be creative, do something different, brainstorm, use big pictures, include student work, and use a little humor. Hey, it's your ad, be an agency.

A Good Story to Listen To

Once I overheard a coach tell gossiping teachers, in the middle of their gossiping session, that he does not participate in talking about others. This stopped the two gossips in their tracks right then and there. The coach's interjection was effective without being aggressive.

Lesson - all stories should not be shared.

Baby It's Cold Outside
{anecdote}

Okay, it may have been a little nippy outside, but I had to get the students out of the room to burn off some energy. Of course, Mr. Parent called afterward, asking what I was doing taking them outside. I said, *I'm glad you called—did you know Joey was failing social studies?* Suddenly, Mr. Parent had forgotten about the weather.

Lesson - Parent involvement can always be positive.

Bad Hair Day

Everyone is entitled to one bad hair day. This is a day where you just need some space. Alright, now load that board up with work. Then refuse to answer questions. Instead refer them to your secretary. . .who isn't in.

Lesson: Notice I said ONE and grade all the work given

Bankruptcy

After years of teaching in your back pocket, you realize you cannot buy all the extra items for your room. Have students use bulletin board paper and cardboard {that you have collected on the weekend}. Ask for old magazines from colleagues and parents. The IRS lets you write off some "chump change", but get serious, you do have a life and family to take care of too.

Be Caught In Children's Books

It might look odd to see a grown man in the children's book section of the library or book store, but the most creative people write children's books and many times your best ideas erupt from them. Take Chris, for example, who said, "I can think of no more intensely soul-searching time than young adulthood." The key is using cutting edge books, golden books and books that make kids think. Try incorporating the books into a lesson!

Being Flexible Is Not Just for Physical Education

Never forget, you are not the only one in the room. These kids bring an assortment of ideas and experiences with them as they enter the door. Be open to being a participant instead of the person in charge. Also, be able to laugh at yourself. I know you're a gifted and talented teacher, every teacher is, but who said you know everything?

Before Backpacks

New teachers: Always "pack" your materials and manuals for the next day before you leave to go home. It really impresses your principal, fellow teachers and is so helpful if you need a substitute. You seem like a real go-getter, prepping all night for the next day. Hopefully, you will be able to follow through with all the "packing".

Bench Me

A child wants to talk to you at recess, do not be one of those teachers who says go on and play it is recess. Instead, engage with them if they need to talk, even if it is recess. They could always come by the bench to talk and this way it is not during class time. Are you really too busy to be involved with your students and what is going on in their lives? How about a pep talk?

What Is Your Best Lesson?

Know your best lessons. You know, the ones that leave the principal's mouth wide open and even better the ones that make the student's eyes light up. For example, I love having the kids read two books at the same time. You have two readers take turns reading from two different books and the rest of the kids take notes-absorbing two books at once. Then, after they are finished reading, they compare and contrast the two books. Talking about developing good listening skills!

Bestsellers

Consistently talk to your students about reading. Model reading. Ask students what book they are reading. Acknowledge them when you see them in library. Tell them they can use dead time as reading time, like when they are waiting in the car, in the doctor's office or when riding the bus. Encourage them to read in the hallway while they are in line. Reward them by telling them they can have a Coke on you if you catch them reading in the community. Of course, they'll "holler" at you anywhere they see you and some might even fake reading books just to get the Coke, but that's okay. It's worth it to make them think about reading. Sell reading, you are the bestseller.

The Heart of Your Job

You are their G/T teacher, and you know them better than anyone—or at least you should. Their problems are your problems. They cannot perform at their peak and carry old baggage at the same time. Help them see the light, or find a different way of looking at their problems. This is the heart of your job.

Be Yourself
Mirror, Mirror on the Wall

Always be yourself and use gifts and talents that are unique to you as a teacher. Please do not carbon copy the teacher next door. Also, you are not the photograph in the teacher's manual. Learn to laugh at yourself. Know that it is okay to be different. Shakespeare's Polonius said it best, "To thine own self be true."

Outrunning the Competition

As the G/T teacher, it goes with the territory to be different. Model being different in your actions and in your words. Keep your students guessing. Just when they think they have figured you out, it is time to change. This is fast-paced and you must outrun the competition.

Go Hallmark on Them

The Christmas Door Contest is the ultimate challenge for teachers. You must outwit, out think, and out plan all your fellow teachers. I mean, this is blood money. Be creative. Go Hallmark on them. Look at cards. One year, I lost with a musical door. A fellow teacher had decorated an entire wall and had students coming out singing as a choir.

Box or Bag It Rule

Cardboard plus duct tape can become anything. Your students just need a little imagination and they can create masterpieces-large and small. A little hot glue and paper bags can also be a plus. Digging for cardboard can become your #1 weekend hobby, if you're not careful.

Breaking Rules

It seems everyone has standard rules. Raise your hand, use listening ears, speak with inside voices. That's great if you are a standard teacher. But if you are not, create rules that suit your classroom.

1. READ everything.
2. Be nice to everyone.
3. Be a thinker.
4. Be creative.
5. Be a risk taker.
6. Be different.

Cure for the Messy Desk

Of course, you have those kids whose desks look like they could endanger you if you stuck your hand anywhere near them. Offer a prize for the "best" desk. Miss Organized will be surprised, yes, and yes, Miss Organized will win. Mr. Messy will get the message.

Doctors on Call

You are going to get sick, it is a guarantee. You are literally a germ incubator. Sneezes, coughing, sore throats and of course the dreadful flu will enter your life like never before. When will someone come up with a miracle drug for something for a teacher's immune system? Students are now taught to take a sleeve- it just so happens that the sleeves aren't long enough for the germs. Sick days, use them. If you try to save them you will end up using more just to get well. Don't risk kicking off to save those golden sick days, you are probably not going to ever get that bonus money when you retire. We just need a doctor on call.

Door Contest No. 2
{anecdote}

I had my grits handed to me last year in Christmas Door Contest - the one with the entire wall and live choir. I wanted to win the contest badly this time, no holds barred. I brought out the cardboard, built a storefront on the door and got the kids to help build cardboard toys to put on the shelves. I won this time!

Lesson - Never give up, keep on keeping on.

Double Dip

Always be looking for opportunities for your students to conquer two concepts or objectives in one setting. If you have a writing assignment, make it about someone in the community which allows them to use research skills and maybe communication skills. Another idea would be to use their writing talents to enter local contests or to try to sell themselves for a job.

Face It

Face it, every classroom has a kid who loves to make those weird faces. Knowing which student that is will especially come in handy when you have a unit on animals. Put the student in charge of animal faces to liven up the unit and get those facial expressions released at the right time. Win, Win!

Fake It So You Can Take It

Some days you just have to get away from it all. They are called Mental Health Days. You can't call in for a mental heath day, so you will have to be sick. A cough is necessary when you call in. Beware, though, do not go out in the community. Escape to the couch and relax. You can even catch up on the dishes. That MHD will put you back on track to be your best self for many days to come.

Fearless

Do not be afraid to develop relationships with your students. Good teachers develop mutual respect and care for their students. Many feel if they loosen up they will lose control of the classroom. The great teachers are not afraid to let their guard down based on their understanding of the relationship. Not all will respond to this, but 99% will.

Up and At "Em"

Use your kids to teach! They can be great manipulatives. That is, they can use their own bodies to demonstrate concepts they're learning. They can make great human bar graphs, number lines, segments, flowers, and more. Kids love this type of lesson and it gets them out of their seats and moving in a positive way.

Fouled Out

As you grow older or wiser some rules must be held tight and some can be relaxed. A good teacher who is also a coach/referee knows the difference between when to call a foul or when to let play continue in the classroom.

Gilligan's Island

Do not get self-absorbed in your own classroom. No one can be an island. If you do not build bridges with others, you will find yourself isolated. No one wants a top biller on their team. It takes Gilligan, the skipper too and all the rest!

The Golden Rule

Make friends with everyone. And I mean everyone. Be smart. No one needs enemies. Tell the cafeteria workers what a great lunch they have prepared and mean it. Your colleagues will be amazed at your portions compared to theirs. Kindness to those in charge of the supply closet will almost always guarantee that your supplies will not run low. The custodian is normally one of the nicest employees in the building, make him/her your best bud. Work smarter, not harder. Treat everyone the way you want to be treated.

Go to the Extra Mile

You're having a dinner party, but you have a student who is having a piano recital and has asked you to come during the same time as your party. Her dad is military and on duty overseas. Excuse yourself, leave the party, get in the car and go the extra mile to attend the recital. You will be forgiven. This applies even if it is Sunday afternoon naptime. If a child is in a play, attend the play. Attend the tennis match even if it is a hot May afternoon. If your students ask you to attend their extra-curricular activities, try your hardest to go the extra mile.

Go to the Corner

Being put in the corner is not always a bad thing. Go to one of the corners and speak softly so that the children will be drawn to the corner with you. You can also use this technique when returning from recess when students are still on the rowdy side. Corner teaching will help you gain control quickly. It never hurts to do something different even if it means being put in the corner.

Pat on the Back

When your lessons are flowing well, try this. Praise a child for an answer or for a great performance by including their classmates in the praise. Say great job _____ {name} and have the class repeat your praise saying it all together several times. It makes all the students feel great and really calls attention to a good answer or performance.

Hilary's Community

Remember, you are not the number one source of information on life, teaching, and wisdom—EVEN if you have mastered three-digit division. When you have the opportunity to listen to a guest speaker, do so. Each guest to your room is important and their knowledge is invaluable. An example, an older gentleman came in and talked about his woodworking hobby. When asked why he didn't sell his art, he said if he was paid for it, it would become a job and he wouldn't enjoy it anymore. If I had been grading papers instead of listening to him that day, I would have missed a valuable lesson myself.

Ho, Ho, Ho

Christmas will roll around quicker than you think. Your gift to your student should be unique. Make something in advance and personalize it in some way. Try to stay away from the Dollar Store just this time. They will probably always remember that gift. Also, I hope you love chocolates and coffee cups because a lot of those will be coming your way!

Incorporate, Incorporate, Incorporate

There may be a "set in stone" curriculum, but that does not mean you cannot incorporate your lessons with other events, people, places, or even things. Knowing where the Gateway Arch is located and what it stands for or what the Everglades are or why John Glenn is famous can easily be incorporated in all curriculum. Always give your students more than what is set in stone.

Hot Off the Press

You are doing a great job as a teacher and you get your picture on the front page of the local paper. You look good and doing your thing with the kids at the teacher's fair, it hits the press. As an added plus your principal is standing beside you in the picture. Do not let your head get too big for your hat. Do not get too full of yourself if you want to see yourself and your students spotlighted again.

IRA

The PTSO {Parent Teacher Student Organization} is generously handing out classroom checks. Take it and spend it even if you don't need classroom supplies at the time. The day will come you will need them. Too bad the money can not go into an IRA.

It Is Okay to Cry

When you have a student cry over a test grade {it could even be a B}, you know that student is a winner. Tell them how proud you are that they care enough about their grades to get emotional and how proud you are of them.

Attention Kmart Shoppers

Teachers, you are a public figure at all times. Remember that your students might notice you anywhere in the community. So, when it comes to buying certain items or refreshments, you might not want to buy them in your community. As a general rule, only do things in your community that you would be comfortable with your students seeing you do!

Look My Way

There are many reasons students are hesitant about making eye contact with you. They can be nervous about speaking in front of the class or unsure of their ability to answer questions correctly. Even if a student doesn't want to be engaged, you won't build their confidence by not calling on them. Give them a chance for success and call on them occasionally. Both you and your student might be surprised. Another way to provide confidence is to tell a very shy child that you are going to call on them for question #3 so they can prepare ahead of time.

Lounges Are for Nights

Do not spend a lot of time in the teacher's lounge. It makes you look like you are not busy and you will find that negative talk is contagious; so, it is best to avoid it. Just drop in and wish all a good day, but don't get caught lounging.

Maytag Moment

It is wise to keep an extra set of clothes with you at school. This can come in handy, playing water balloons with your students can often result in wet pants. Bottoms up!

Moment by Moment

The best teachers are always teaching and finding teachable moments in all situations. The moments can present themselves at recess, in the cafeteria, the hallway or any place in school. The best teachers find ways to make connections for their students by asking questions that reinforce content from the classroom. Especially on field trips, make those connections.

Examples: *Find all the squares in the hallway. What kinds of clouds do you see?*

Change of Command

A change of principal can be dangerous to your health. Okay, so you had a principal who let you do things your way and now that has changed. The best of advice to make it with a very disciplined principal is TO STAY UNDER THE RADAR!

Next Best Lesson

"The Three Questions" from Tolstoy's short story are good rules to live by. First, who is the most important person? The person you are with right now. Second, what is the most important time? Right now. Third, what is the most important thing to do? Do right by this person. Keep these rules in mind with your students and teach them valuable life lessons.

Pay Pal

When it comes to getting your paychecks, prepare yourself for a harrowing experience. It is best to open your payroll stub while in a seated position. Of course, you were hired knowing you were getting a huge salary, but what happened? Looks like you are a philanthropist instead of a classroom teacher. You are giving to everyone and everything: city, state, Feds, teacher's union, retirement and even some school fees. *Sorry, this is your deposit until next month and it will be the same thing over again.* Pay Pal? We don't do it for the money.

Photo Bomb

It's always picture day at school. The local paper features everything: the DAR, sports, contests, 4-H, speech, academic teams. Odyssey of the Mind, KYA, winners and losers in little league, musical and drama events, you name it and a picture will be taken. That is a good thing! No one wants you taking up space in front of their child's moment in time. Stand in the back. It doesn't matter if you are in the picture. Most importantly, make sure all names are spelled correctly in the captions!

Raise That Bar

It doesn't matter what the subject, what event, or what time, find a way to raise the bar for your students. Aim straight for the sky. Look for connections, patterns, experiences and ask tough high-level questions. Believe me, your students will rise to the occasion. Be sure not to overdo it though. Find the right amount of challenge for each child. Your job is to build them up, not tear them down. Help them raise the bar and reach their potential.

Read Those Folders

Take your time and read those folders. Don't just read but study each child's folder. Know their names before they enter the room. Know what makes them tick. Get a grasp on their areas of potential. Look for those left behind and what caused it. You cannot solve problems if you do not know what they are. Look at all notes, scores and any other data you have available, especially if the student started off well and then slumped. But most importantly, the past does not dictate the future! It is a bright new day when a child enters your classroom with a clean slate. You form judgements based upon your relationship, not on their past records. Use those folders only to understand them.

Red Mulch Needed

Every teacher encounters the child with the 'I believe I may be getting sick' look. First, it is already too late to get out of the way. Prepare for the fluid to head your way. Now if you are lucky and grabbed the trash can, great. If it landed on you, well, it's just part of the job. But the rule says to tell the class we are okay even while everyone is screaming "yuck." Red cedar, here we come!

Root Canal

I know it can be painful, like a root canal, but be willing to listen to others. There might be a bit of wisdom in what they are saying. You might be inspired to become a reader, a better learner, or get yourself better organized. You might even learn new vocabulary words. Then head for a pleasant experience like a root canal.

Roses, Anyone?

Even in the midst of constant teaching, tests, and all the stress, you must remind yourself that there are times to stop and smell the roses. Stop and call attention when a child does something really nice for you or others no matter how small the gesture. This is a great mini lesson in kindness and caring. *Great job, Tom/Teresa!*

Rule: Watch Those Emails

You've sent the email. Okay, you said it, now what are you going to do? Email is a written record of what you said, and your words can be misconstrued, especially tone. Just be careful, try friendly conversation the next time unless you need documentation.

R U Listening?

Children/students, they will not always find what you are teaching as interesting. In fact, you will never have 100% of a student's attention at any time. The key is not to talk until everyone is focused. Use techniques to get their attention. Try varying your tones, whisper or talk at a medium volume, or don't talk at all. Instead communicate with signals. This is a really good strategy for gaining the attention of the class. It's your job to get them to listen.

Quiet Mouse

Whenever your class is getting a little out of hand or just too noisy, try the pin trick. It is an incentive for good behavior. Ask the class to be part of an experiment to see if they can be quiet enough to be able to hear a pin drop on the floor. Once the pin drops, they will be able to hear it if they are quiet enough. Keep trying until everyone hears it. Hint: make sure you don't drop the pin on the carpet, teacher!

Let Their Voices Be Heard

ALWAYS encourage your students to use their voices to speak out, answer questions, teach a lesson, give a report or interview. Encourage them to get up in front of the class. This builds self-confidence and self-esteem in each child.

Starbucks

Check out your image daily. Put that shirt with a missing button back in the closet. Remember, coffee stains, spots and missing buttons are just shout-outs from your students waiting to happen. And don't forget to be careful with that morning coffee in the car! You can earn "Star Bucks" by being on your style game everyday.

Table for Four

When everything else fails, go to grouping. Grouping can be a discipline system beyond compare and is also great for competition. Be careful with your groupings. Know your students well and pick compatible students to sit at a table for four. Then let the games begin. Have them compete to be the first group to engage the class, the first group to clean up the room, the quietest group or you name it.

Take One for the Team

Become the sacrificial lamb. Everyone will at one time or another have to make a sacrifice for the school or for the good of the team. Yes, you will have to forget your ego, self-esteem and vanity-just do it! Dress the crazy part, sleep on the roof for charity, play the crazy games in the gym, take a pie in the face or even kiss the pig. Just be careful, you know the pigs do have teeth. The kids will squeal with delight.

Take the Trash Out, Bring the Trash In

Sometimes it is better to bring the trash in instead of taking it out. Be constantly looking for items that have been discarded. Be careful in using your new-found treasures and use them in your classroom in new ways.

Sub Way

You will find that everyone needs a substitute for their class at some point. Now subs come in all shapes, forms, sizes and personalities. Be smart if you have a choice in your substitute. You do not want Mr. or Mrs. Nice and Easygoing. Students love that sub, but not much gets accomplished. Here is the solution. Request the "meanest" sub available. When I say mean, use the student's definition of mean. The students will love you all the more when you return.

Thinking Skills

Thinking skills are some of the most important skills to be taught. This is important for left and right brainers. Thorough answers come by waiting and evaluating questions instead of using first thought. Learning to look for patterns in various situations is not only for math and science but all areas of study. Problem solving can be taught by using different strategies. Teach your students how to work through logic problems, don't just expect them to know how to do them. Teach them to think futuristic. Teach them how to develop answers to problems. Incorporate the right brain into the logical left brain whenever you can. Thinking skills are some of the most important to teach but can also be the hardest but most rewarding for the teacher and the student.

Those Short Faculty Meetings {anecdote}

Who in the world wants to sit through a faculty meeting? Someone else is usually telling you how to teach. The cure - bring a good book, daydream or text if you can, just make sure you don't get caught. Make sure you look engaged and complete your paperwork. Most of all, make sure you sign in!

Trash It or Keep It

Here's a trick to try when a student leaves their name off of their paper. Once you figure out who the paper belongs to, tell the student they have a 50/50 shot of getting it back. Hold the paper over a trash can. If it falls in, tell the student it stays there, but if it flies by, you're safe. *Just Kidding*, you then tell them! Try it for a laugh and to discourage them from forgetting to put their name on the paper again.

Tutoring

There is a child that needs tutoring. To get the job done, you may need those extra books and materials but just maybe you have the skills and ideas to help the child conquer the subject matter. For any child, here's a super tip: tutor for the future as well as what they have not mastered. Don't play catch up, play go ahead. This way, the child can build confidence.

Wranglers Recommended

Ladies and gentlemen, there will come a time when you have to teach by the seat of your pants. Literally, your pants will split and there will be nowhere to go. Solution - find a sweater or jacket and tie it around your waist. Tell them it is fashionable. *See Maytag Moments for similar situations.*

Your Room

Remember your room growing up, most people do. The colors, the special awards, the heirloom teddy bears and everything else that made it special. Well, the classroom is not yours, it belongs to everyone that shares it with you. Create a room that is kid friendly with an atmosphere that says, *we are family and we do not harm or bring each other down.* The walls are teaching tools in the making. Create your own posters. Put visuals at eye level, write encouraging notes to your kids, bring things that makes your room unique. Make it a special place. It is not a dentist's office.

You Think??

To me, the most important thing you can teach your student is the ability to think creatively. Creativity can be taught! Over time, you can help your students develop creative skills by teaching them to brainstorm and piggy back. Point out the novel or unusual in their schoolwork. Teach pattern recognition in all subjects. Make comments and connections to other subjects and life. Encourage positivity in all situations and always keep asking high-level questions.

You've Got Talent

Always spotlight your kids. It doesn't have to be Broadway, it can just be an everyday. It is their show, not yours. How about having a "daily actor" activity? Have a different student dress and become a famous historical figure each day. You'll see some real talent!

You Want Proof

Do not be so sure that a given student has not studied their coursework. Imagine your surprise when the student brings in an actual photograph of them studying your textbook! It will qualify as Exhibit A in the classroom.

ABOUT THE AUTHOR

James Redd is a retired elementary and gifted/talented teacher where he taught in many school districts in Western Kentucky. He prided himself in being unconventional and pushed himself to find unique and creative ways to teach his students based on caring and mutual respect.

He coached Odyssey of the Mind, Academic, and Stock Market Teams. His students and teams received many state awards.

This book reflects what his students taught him along the way. It also reflects the observations he made of his peers and the teaching profession in general. This book is based on his love for the art of teaching more than any other profession.